FELT INLAYS

**Creative Publishing
international**

First published in the United States of America by
Creative Publishing international, Inc., a member of
Quayside Publishing Group
400 First Avenue North
Suite 300
Minneapolis, MN 55401
1-800-328-3895
www.creativepub.com

ISBN-13: 978-1-58923-362-1
ISBN-10: 1-58923-362-X

10 9 8 7 6 5 4 3 2 1

Library of Congress Cataloging-in-Publication Data
Hoerner, Nancy.
  Felt inlays : making textured and patterned felt for 23 creative projects /
Nancy Hoerner.
      p. cm.
  ISBN 1-58923-362-X
  1. Felting. 2. Felt work. I. Title.

  TT849.5.H745 2008
  746'.0463--dc22   2007049073
                                                      CIP

Copy Editor: Catherine Broberg
Proofreader: Andrea Schein
Cover and Book Design: Indicia Design
Page Layout: Indicia Design

Printed in Singapore

FELT
INLAYS

Making Textured and Patterned Felt for 23 Creative Projects

NANCY HOERNER

Creative Publishing
international

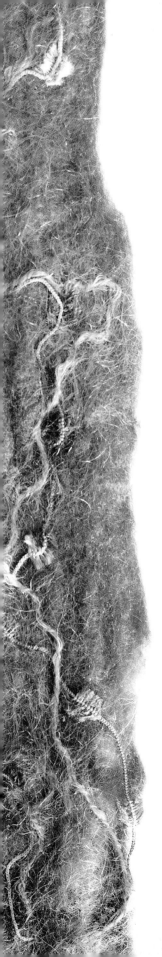

CONTENTS

Introduction

Like many crafters, you may have experimented with wet felting—adding soapy water to layers of wool roving and agitating them until they mat together into fabric. If you've never tried wet felting, follow the instructions on page 13, and you'll catch on quickly. When you plan your design with selective colors and catch additional materials into the fabric, you create felt inlays. It's fun to do and the resulting fabric is always soft and beautiful.

In this book, I'll show you how to carry the inlay felting technique to new heights. You will see many colorful inlays on these pages that incorporate yarns, prefelts, an array of fibers, and other possibilities. While all inlays contain wool, many of them blend wool with other fibers that cannot felt on their own. As the wool fibers felt together, they lock the other materials in place. For even more impressive results, some inlays are embellished with stitching by hand or machine, ribbon embroidery, and beads.

But why stop there? Felt inlays can be used to make all kinds of useful and decorative items for gift-giving, fashion, and home décor. You can use them to create purses and bags, to cover books and journals, and to make jewelry. These projects and more are included in this book. The project chapters are arranged by the type of material being worked into the inlay, with the easiest materials first and progressing to more challenging materials.

The inlays, and thus the projects, are small so you don't need a large space to work. I make my felt inlays on the kitchen counter next to the sink and close to the microwave. Make your inlays as large as your working mat will allow so that you have plenty of the finished fabric to work with. If you wish to make a project that requires more felt, simply make two or more pieces. Joining pieces is easy because cut edges of felt do not fray. Seam allowances can be hidden on the inside or visible on the outside, whichever you prefer.

Every felt inlay you create is an adventure. The minute details of the design cannot be controlled—motifs can distort and shift during the felting process—yet such unpredictability is exactly what leads to unique creations. When you understand the limits and possibilities, you'll be prepared for pleasant surprises every time!

I hope you will share my enthusiasm for inlaid felting and will experiment with different materials. With this medium, the sky is the limit.

nancy

BASIC FELTING

Felting is a simple, three-stage process. It doesn't require high-tech, expensive tools, only items you probably have around the house or can find in the housewares department of your nearby store. Perhaps the only material you will have to buy is the wool roving. In stage one, you arrange the roving in thin layers, alternating directions. Water, soap, and agitation cause the wool fibers to cling to each other—felting stage— and form a dense, matted fabric—fulling stage. Artistic and versatile, this fabric doesn't fray or ravel and it can be used for anything from home décor items to clothing.

Materials

Wool roving is wool that has been carded to align the fibers. This is the stage of preparation before the wool is spun into yarn. Roving comes as a fluffy rope and is purchased by the ounce (gram). Most projects in this book require 2 to 3 oz. (56.7 to 85 g) of roving. You can buy roving dyed in solid colors **(1)**, variegated (dyed one color with different shades throughout) **(2)**, or hand-painted (dyed with several colors along the rope) **(3)**.

Soap is an important element in felting and the inlay process. Soap allows your hands to slide over the felt surface easily. Kiss My Face olive oil soap **(4)** is one of the best brands to use but I have also found Dawn dish soap to work well. The olive oil soap, available at health food stores, comes in a bar and must be shredded. When you mix it with water, it forms a gel.

Water is a necessity, and some felters think that it must be hot. I use both lukewarm and hot water. Mix the soap and water in a quart container **(5)** and pour it into a plastic squirt bottle **(6)** to apply it to the roving.

A bamboo or reed mat **(7)**, such as a common placemat, is used to roll up the felt during the fulling stage. You can also use bubble wrap with small bubbles and roll it up bubble-side out. Rubber bands keep the rolled mat together.

You will need net fabric **(8)**—mosquito netting or curtain material—cut to the size of the mat.

Bath towels **(9)** provide a nice textured rolling surface and keep the water from running onto the floor.

Use a plastic tray **(10)** large enough to hold the bamboo mat while you are wetting the roving.

For cutting straight edges for your projects, use a rotary cutter, mat, and ruler **(11)**.

You may need a single-edge razor blade **(12)** for making small cuts (such as buttonholes) or slices from felt snakes.

Directions for Basic Felting

Arranging the roving

1. Place a large towel on your work surface, then the mat on a plastic tray. It is best if the work area is near a water source and a heat source. A kitchen counter usually works well, as it is near the sink and the microwave, which is used for heating water. This setting also accommodates the small size of these projects quite well.

2. Fluff up the end of the roving and pull out a tuft of fiber. Place the tuft a couple of inches (centimeters) from the end of the mat and a couple of inches (centimeters) down from the top.

3. Repeat step 2, placing the tufts in a horizontal row with edges touching. Place a second row of fibers partially overlapping the first row, like shingles on a roof. Place as many rows as needed to fill in the area across the mat and to within a couple of inches (centimeters) from all sides. This is the first of three layers.

4. Apply layer two in rows perpendicular to the first layer.

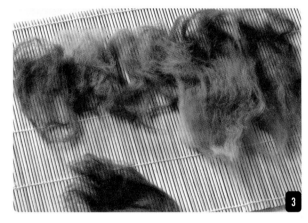

TIP: Alternate the colors of roving in each layer for interesting results. Because the layers are very thin, the fibers will blend together when felted.

5. Apply layer three in rows perpendicular to the second layer.

6. Cover the layers with the net fabric and place as much of the mat as possible into the tray.

Felting stage

1. Shred a bar of olive oil soap and place it in a quart bottle. Fill the bottle with hot water and let it sit for a day or two until a gel forms and the soap shreds are dissolved.

2. Put a tablespoon of the gel (or liquid dish soap) in a quart bottle. Fill the bottle with hot water. Pour the solution into a squirt bottle.

3. Remove the net and squirt the fibers with the soap solution until they are soaked thoroughly. Gently press out any air bubbles, working from the center to the sides with the palm of your hand. Tuck in any thin fibers along the sides to make an even edge.

4. Replace the net and rub very gently in circles across the surface using more soapy water, as necessary, to lubricate the fibers. Rub for about fifteen minutes. The fibers will begin to felt together.

(continued)

Directions for Basic Felting (continued)

The inlay process

The inlay process starts between the felting and fulling stages. Before rolling the layers, arrange inlay materials on the surface of the felt and wet them down. Then continue with step 1 of the fulling stage and the materials will felt into the background. It's as easy as that!

TIP: Rewarm the soap solution occasionally in the microwave.

Fulling stage

1. Roll up the mat, fibers, and net and secure the roll with rubber bands near the ends. Remove the tray from your work surface and pour any remaining solution back into the bottle for use at another time.

2. Lay the roll on a towel and roll it back and forth 100 times. In this fulling stage, the fibers will shrink, making the piece thicken and become harder.

3. Open the roll and turn the felt piece 90 degrees. Smooth out the fabric and roll it back up. Roll the rolled mat over the towel 100 times more.

4. Repeat step 3 at least twice more, until the felt has become hard and will not change shape easily.

5. Remove the felt piece from the roll and rinse it in cold tap water to remove the soap.

6. Roll up the felt in a dry towel to squeeze out excess water. Smooth the piece and lay it out to dry.

YARN INLAYS

Yarns are easy and fun to work into a stunning design. There are many wool yarns on the market. Those that are 100 percent wool felt in the best, but even yarns that have only 60 percent wool work very nicely. Novelty yarns, on the other hand, often don't have any wool in them but they will still felt in if they are fuzzy or hairy. The wool fibers will grab hold of the fine fibers and bond.

Flamenco Purse

This little red purse can go anywhere and people will ask if you made it. What fun to show off your style, good taste, and artistic flair.

Directions

Making the felt inlay

1. Following steps 1 to 6 on pages 12–13, arrange the red wool roving in a 14" x 8" (35.6 x 20.3 cm) area.

2. Follow steps 1 to 4 of the felting stage on page 13.

3. Remove the net. Arrange the yarn in a looping pattern. Using the squirt bottle, wet the yarn and gently press it into place.

4. Follow steps 1 to 6 of the fulling stage on page 15.

5. Repeat steps 1 to 4 above to make a second piece.

(continued)

Materials

- felting equipment
- variegated wool roving in red
- super bulky wool yarn in bright pinks, orange, and fuchsia color range (we used Fettuccini by Lion Brand, color Starburst)
- rotary cutter, mat, and ruler
- sewing machine
- red thread and needle
- iron and press cloth

Flamenco Purse (continued)

Making a felt bead

1. Make a ball from a small piece of wool roving and wet it. Roll it around in the palm of your hand, adding soap when needed.

2. Gradually increase the size of the bead by adding fine strands of roving a little at a time until the bead is the desired size.

3. Continue to felt the bead until it is hard. Rinse it and then set it aside to dry.

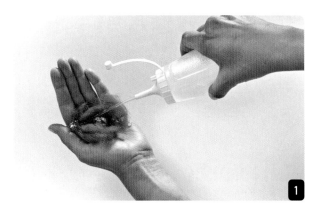

Variation: To make a multicolor half bead, for use as a button or embellishment, follow the bead directions but add layers of different colors. When the bead is sliced in half, the different layers will show and make an interesting embellishment.

Making a felt braid

1. Form two strands of roving 28" (71.1 cm) long by gently rolling the roving between your palms. Cut a piece of yarn the same length. Tie the three strands together 5" (12.7 cm) from one end. Braid the strands to within 5" (12.7 cm) of the opposite end. Tie another knot.

2. Wet the braid with soapy water, either by squirting it or by dipping it, leaving the ends dry. Place the braid in a fold of the bamboo mat and roll it until the braid is felted. Check your progress frequently and add more soapy water, if necessary.

3. Divide the dry strands on each end if they have become entangled. Wet each strand and roll it in your hands until it is felted.

4. Rinse out excess soap and set the braid aside to dry.

Making the flamenco purse

1. Using the rotary cutter, mat, and ruler, cut one piece of the felt inlay 8½" x 6¾" (21.6 x 17.2 cm) with straight cuts on all sides. Cut the second piece 11½" x 6¾" (29.2 x 17.2 cm), leaving one short end with its natural edge.

2. Layer the pieces right sides together, aligning the straight short ends and sides. The natural short end will extend above. Machine-stitch the three sides with a ⅜" (1 cm) seam, rounding the corners at the bottom.

3. Turn the purse right side out and turn the flap down. Press, using a pressing cloth.

4. Cut a slit in the center of the flap just long enough to fit over the bead. Sew the bead in place on the bag front under the slit.

5. Sew the knots of the felt braid handle to the purse sides, staggering the heights if desired.

TIP: If some of the yarn is not attached very well, secure it with fabric adhesive.

Materials

- felting equipment
- hand-painted wool roving in aqua to purple color range
- super bulky wool yarn in blue and green (we used Fettuccini by Lion Brand)
- novelty yarns in blue and turquoise
- rotary cutter, mat, and ruler
- sewing machine
- fused glass button, ¾" (1.9 cm) square or felted button
- iron and press cloth

Turquoise Jewelry Bag

This unique little bag is fun to make and handy to take on your next trip. Use it to keep your jewelry from getting lost or scratched in the shuffle.

Directions

Making the felt inlay

1. Following steps 1 to 6 on pages 12–13, arrange the aqua and purple wool roving in a 16" x 8" (40.6 x 20.3 cm) area.

2. Follow steps 1 to 4 of the felting stage on page 13.

3. Remove the net. Arrange the wool yarn diagonally 2" (5.1 cm) apart across the wet fibers; arrange the novelty yarn horizontally 2" (5.1 cm) apart over the fibers. Spritz the yarn and gently press it into place.

4. Follow steps 1 to 6 of the fulling stage on page 15.

Making the jewelry bag

1. Using the rotary cutter, mat, and ruler, trim the two long sides and one short side of the felt inlay, leaving one short end with its natural edge.

2. Fold up the straight-cut end about 5" (12.7 cm), wrong sides together, to form a pocket. The flap with the natural edge should extend about 3" (7.6 cm) beyond the straight edge. Machine-stitch the two sides with a ⅜" (1 cm) seam.

3. Cut a slit in the center of the flap, ½" (1.3 cm) from the edge, long enough to accommodate your button.

4. Turn the flap down. Press, using a press cloth.

5. Make a slit on the flap to fit the button. Sew the button in place on the bag front under the slit.

TIP: Alternate the colors of roving in each layer for interesting results. Because the layers are very thin, the fibers will blend together when felted.

Materials

- felting equipment
- hand-painted wool roving in purple to rust color range
- variegated yarn in blue and purple (we used Rag Dolls from Red Heart, color 5336 Hop)
- sapphire seed beads
- blue beading thread and needle
- rotary cutter, mat, and ruler
- sewing machine

Handy Tissue Holder

Need a tissue? Even in a dark theater, you can reach into your purse and easily locate this soft, felt inlay holder. A few seed beads, added to accent the inlaid yarn, make this handy little item a piece you'll want to show off.

Directions

Making the felt inlay

1. Following steps 1 to 6 on pages 12–13, arrange the hand-painted wool roving in an 8" (20.3 cm) square area.

2. Follow steps 1 to 4 of the felting stage on page 13.

3. Remove the net. Arrange the yarn randomly. Using the squirt bottle, wet the yarn and gently press it into place.

4. Follow steps 1 to 6 of the fulling stage on page 15.

Making the tissue holder

1. Using the rotary cutter, mat, and ruler, cut one piece of the felt inlay 3" x 5" (7.6 x 12.7 cm) and two pieces 3" x 2½" (7.6 x 6.4 cm).

2. With the blue beading thread and a needle, sew blue beads along the edges of the inlaid yarn for an accent. Bead only on the two small pieces.

3. Layer the two small pieces over the large piece, right sides together, with the two small pieces abutting each other. Machine-stitch around the outside with a ⅜" (1 cm) seam. See photo below.

4. Turn the holder right side out and insert a pocket-size package of tissues.

Materials

- felting equipment

- wool roving in red, coral, orange, pink, and yellow

- super bulky wool yarn in bright pinks, orange, and fuchsia color range (we used Fettuccini by Lion Brand, color Starburst)

- sewing needle and thread

- sewing machine

- dark ruby, silver-lined seed beads

- red beading thread and needle

- rotary cutter, mat, and ruler

- snap

Confetti Coin Purse

Loose change never had such a classy home. Instead of jangling around in the bottom of your tote, those elusive quarters and dimes will be easier to find in your felt inlay coin purse.

Directions

Making the felt inlay

1. Following steps 1 to 6 on page 12, arrange the wool on the mat. For the top layer, use pieces of all five colors.

2. Follow steps 1 to 4 of the felting stage on page 13.

3. Remove the net. Cut 1" (2.5 cm) pieces of the yarn and scatter them over the surface. Using the squirt bottle, wet the yarn and gently press it into place.

4. Follow steps 1 to 6 of the fulling stage on page 15.

Making the coin purse

1. Using the rotary cutter, mat, and ruler, cut a piece of felt inlay 9" x 3" (22.9 x 7.6 cm), leaving one short end with its natural edge.

2. Fold up the straight-cut end about 3" (7.6 cm), wrong sides together, to form a pocket. The flap with the natural edge should extend about 3" (7.6 cm) beyond the straight edge. Machine-stitch the two sides with a ⅜" (1 cm) seam.

3. With the red beading thread and a needle, sew ruby beads along the edges of the yarn pieces on the flap, spacing the beads about ⅛" (3 mm) apart.

4. Hand-sew the socket part of the snap to the right side of the underlap, about ½" (1.3 cm) below the edge. Sew the ball part of the snap to the wrong side of the flap, aligning it to the socket.

Materials

- felting equipment
- wool roving in red, coral, orange, pink, and yellow
- super bulky wool yarn in bright pinks, orange, and fuchsia color range (we used Fettuccini by Lion Brand, color Starburst)
- fuchsia-lined crystal seed beads
- red beading thread and needle
- rotary cutter, mat, and ruler
- fabric adhesive
- tongue depressor
- plastic sewing kit

Confetti Sewing Kit

Turn a mundane sewing kit into something special by adorning it with a felt inlay cover. I found this little Dritz plastic case sewing kit hanging on the notions wall of the local fabric store. You could use this same idea to fancy up your compact or mirror case, too.

Directions

Making the felt inlay

1. Following steps 1 to 6 on pages 12–13, arrange the wool on the mat. For the top layer, use pieces of all five colors.

2. Follow steps 1 to 4 of the felting stage on page 13.

3. Remove the net. Cut 1" (2.5 cm) pieces of the yarn and scatter them over the surface. Using the squirt bottle, wet the yarn and gently press it into place.

4. Follow steps 1 to 6 of the fulling stage on page 15.

Making the sewing kit cover

1. Using the rotary cutter, mat, and ruler, cut a long strip of the felt inlay the width of the kit. Place the kit on one end of the strip and trim the felt to match. Then wrap the strip over the closed case and mark and cut the opposite end.

2. With the red beading thread and a needle, sew seed beads along the edges of the yarn pieces, spacing the beads about 1⁄8" (3 mm) apart.

3. Spread adhesive on the outside of the kit cover, using a tongue depressor. Adhere the felt to the cover

TIP: When adhering felt inlay to another surface, you'll be more successful and create less mess if you apply the glue to the solid surface.

Beaded Bracelets

Cut a narrow strip from each inlay you make and stockpile them for a fun bracelet-embellishing party. These bracelets are truly original—no two will ever be alike. Even strips cut from the same inlay can be very different from each other.

Directions

Making a bracelet

1. Follow the directions for making any felt inlay piece. Measure around your wrist and cut a strip 1" (2.5 cm) longer than this measurement and 1" or 1¼" (2.5 or 3.2 cm) wide.

2. Sew beads to the right side of the strip, following designs in the inlay or creating patterns of your own. See photo below.

3. Sew the socket side of a large snap to the right side of the bracelet at one end. Sew the ball side of the snap to the underside of the opposite end, lapping the ends 1" (2.5 cm).

2

Beading a flower motif

1. Thread the beading needle. Knot the end and anchor it on the wrong side of the bracelet, bringing the thread through to the front.

2. Thread three seed beads onto the needle and go through to the back slightly beyond the end of the beads.

3. Bring the needle back through to the front ¼" (6 mm) from the end of the beads. Run the needle back through the beads and through the fabric to the back.

4. Bring the needle back to the front a short distance from the first row of beads. Repeat steps 2 and 3 until you've made eight spokes of beads in a flower shape.

More beading ideas

Outline the path of inlaid yarns with seed beads along the sides or through the center of the yarns.

Stitch large beads in open spaces or stitch them in rows around the bracelet.

PREFELT INLAYS

Prefelts are thin, felted layers of wool roving that have not gone through the final fulling stage. You can cut or tear pieces to inlay in your felt for more color and to develop designs. Create your own prefelt or buy solid colors of prefelt ready-made (see Resources, page 96).

To make prefelt, follow steps 1 to 4 of the felting stage (page 13), but lay out only two layers of roving. Then follow steps 1 to 3 of the fulling stage. Unroll the prefelt and let it dry.

When adding prefelts to your inlays, start with geometric shapes until you get the idea of how it works. Expect surprises—the motifs can distort and shift in the felting process. Keep a bag of prefelt scraps on hand. You never know when even the tiniest pieces will come in handy.

Materials

- felting equipment
- hand-painted wool roving in gold and purple
- super bulky wool yarn in bright pinks, orange, and fuchsia color range (we used Fettuccini by Lion Brand, color Starburst)
- prefelts in dark red and gold
- rotary cutter, mat, and ruler

Fiesta Napkin Rings

Jazz up your dining table with these festive napkin rings.
Choose roving, prefelts, and yarns in a family of colors that
will set off your dishes and table linens to perfection.

Directions

Making the felt inlay

1. Following steps 1 to 6 on pages 12–13, arrange the wool roving to cover as much of the mat as possible.

2. Follow steps 1 to 4 of the felting stage on page 13.

3. Remove the net. Arrange the yarn in a looping pattern.

4. Cut several dark red, 1" (2.5 cm) prefelt circles and gold, 1" (2.5 cm) prefelt triangles. Scatter them over the surface. Using the squirt bottle, wet the yarn and prefelt pieces and gently press them into place.

5. Place the net back over the wet layers and rub for fifteen minutes.

6. Follow steps 1 to 6 of the fulling stage on page 15.

Making the napkin rings

1. Using a rotary cutter, mat, and ruler, cut the felt into 10" x 1½" (25.4 x 3.8 cm) strips. See photo below.

2. Cut a slit 1½" (3.8 cm) long 1" (2.5 cm) from one end of each strip.

3. Wrap the napkin rings around a rolled or folded cloth napkin and pull the unslit end through the slit to hold the ring in place.

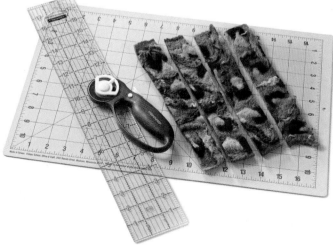

TIP: When you make your own prefelt, work snips of thread, fabric, and ribbons into the fibers for more interesting pattern designs.

Pink Floral Cosmetic Bag

This design takes on more life the longer you work with it. When the pattern of prefelts is laid down on the wet roving layers, it just looks like a bunch of circles and triangles. Once the stitching and beading is done, you'll finally see the flowers. The wisps of silk roving add a beautiful sheen to the inlay.

Directions

Making the felt inlay

1. Cut 15 to 20 pink, 1" (2.5 cm), prefelt circles and the same number of green, 1" (2.5 cm), prefelt triangles. Set them aside.

2. Following steps 1 to 6 on pages 12–13, arrange the wool roving to cover most of the reed mat.

3. Follow steps 1 to 4 of the felting stage on page 13.

4. Remove the net. Arrange the circles in three or four rows over the wet fibers, staggering placement from row to row. Then place a green triangle next to each circle. Tease out wisps of silk roving and place them in the spaces around the motifs. Using the squirt bottle, wet the motifs and silk roving and gently press them into place.

5. Cover the layers with the net and rub for fifteen minutes.

6. Follow steps 1 to 6 of the fulling stage on page 15.

Materials

- felting equipment
- hand-painted wool roving in purple, pink, and gold
- hand-painted silk roving in purple to pink
- prefelts in pink and green
- rotary cutter, mat, and ruler
- sewing needle and green and red sewing threads
- gold seed beads and beading needle or tiny buttons
- iron and press cloth
- sewing machine
- large snap

(continued)

Making the cosmetic bag

1. Using the rotary cutter, mat, and ruler, straighten the two long edges, making them parallel to each other a distance apart equal to the desired width of your bag. Cut one short end straight across; leave the other end with its natural edge.

2. Using red thread, stitch by hand six to eight spokes from the center to the edge of each circle shape to make them look like flowers. Then stitch three gold seed beads or a tiny button in the center of each flower.

3. Using green thread, backstitch down the center and around the edge of each green triangle, making them look like leaves.

4. Fold the piece wrong sides together to make a pocket and flap. Press, using a press cloth.

5. Unfold the flap, and machine-stitch the sides of the pocket with ⅜" (1 cm) seams.

6. Sew the socket part of the snap to the right side of the underlap, about ½" (1.3 cm) below the edge. Sew the ball part of the snap to the wrong side of the flap, aligning it to the socket.

TIP: When you backstitch, pull the thread snug with each stitch. This will give your felt inlays a quilted effect.

Autumn Candle Band

Autumn Candle Band

Accent a pillar candle with a felt band, inlaid with oak leaves and closed with an acorn button. Make your own prefelt for this project, and add some silky fibers for a colorful, textural contrast to the background.

Directions

Making the felt inlay

1. Following the instructions on page 33, make a prefelt of gold wool with gold to orange silk fibers on top.

2. When the prefelt is dry, draw an oak leaf pattern and use it to cut out five prefelt leaves for one band or ten leaves for two bands. Set them aside.

3. Following steps 1 to 6 on pages 12–13, arrange the rust to brown hand-painted wool roving the full length of the mat. Use the full width for two candle wraps or half the width for one.

4. Follow steps 1 to 4 of the felting stage on page 13.

5. Remove the net. Loosely arrange the oak leaves on the wet fiber layers in a single, lengthwise row for one band or in two rows for two bands. Using the squirt bottle, wet the leaves and gently press them into place.

6. Cover the layers with the net and rub for fifteen minutes.

7. Follow steps 1 to 6 of the fulling stage on page 15.

Materials

- felting equipment
- hand-painted wool roving in rust to brown
- prefelt of gold wool with gold to orange silk fibers
- rotary cutter, mat, and ruler
- sewing needle and brown thread
- acorn button
- pillar candle, 8" (20.3 cm) tall, 3" (7.6 cm) diameter

Making the candle band

1. Using the rotary cutter, mat, and ruler, cut one or two bands 12" x 3¼" (30.5 x 8.3 cm). If using a different size candle, measure around the candle and add 1" (2.5 cm) for overlap. Make sure the leaves are centered in the band.

2. Using brown thread, backstitch veins in the leaves.

3. Wrap the band around the candle and overlap the ends so the band fits snugly. Pin. Remove the band and sew an acorn button through both layers of the overlap to hold the band in a circle.

4. Replace the band on the candle and slide it to the desired position.

TIP: Use this idea to make other seasonal candle wraps. How about white prefelt snowflakes on a blue background, or yellow daisies on a green background? Have fun with it. Never leave burning candles unattended.

Pink Daisy Purse

When you only need to carry a few essentials, do it with flair. This sweet little daisy purse is an artful accessory that will have everyone asking, "Where can I get one of those?"

Directions

Making the felt inlay

1. Make a teardrop-shaped pattern, about 2½" (6.4 cm) long and 1½" (3.8 cm) at its widest point, for petals and leaves. Use the pattern to cut out five turquoise prefelt petals and three green prefelt leaves. Set them aside.

2. Following steps 1 to 6 on pages 12–13, arrange the pink wool roving to cover most of the reed mat.

3. Follow steps 1 to 4 of the felting stage on page 13.

4. Remove the net. Arrange the prefelt petals in a circle over the wet fibers, with the tips pointing inward to form the daisy. Place the prefelt leaves between petals, with the tips pointing outward. Using the squirt bottle, wet the motifs and gently press them into place.

5. Cover the layers with the net and rub for fifteen minutes.

6. Follow steps 1 to 6 of the fulling stage on page 15.

7. Make a second felt piece of plain pink for the back of the purse.

Materials

- prefelts in turquoise and green
- felting equipment
- variegated wool roving in pink
- solid wool roving in turquoise and green
- rotary cutter, mat, and ruler
- iron and press cloth
- green embroidery floss or perle cotton and embroidery needle
- 12 pink seed beads
- 12 pink roundel beads
- beading needle and thread
- sewing machine

(continued)

Making the daisy purse

1. Using the rotary cutter, mat, and ruler, cut matching rectangles of the two pieces, about 8" x 7" (20.3 x 17.8 cm) or the size you prefer.

2. Using embroidery floss or perle cotton and an embroidery needle, backstitch veins in the leaves.

3. Stitch a cluster of roundel beads in the center of the flower, using seed beads as stops.

4. Place the purse front and back wrong sides together. Machine-stitch the sides and bottom of the purse, backstitching at the beginning and end.

5. Following the directions on pages 20–21, make a braided handle for the purse, using one strand each of pink, turquoise, and green roving. Sew the handle to the purse.

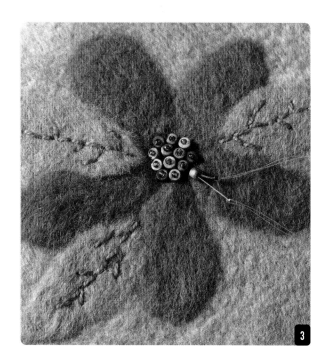

TIP: Let the fibers be your muse! Random patterns of the inlaid yarns create organic designs that just can't be copied. Outlining the yarns with tiny sparkling seed beads gives them more emphasis.

Eye-Catching Glasses Case

Eye-Catching Glasses Case

Felt inlay is the perfect fabric for making a glasses case—it cushions the lenses and protects them from scratches. This case is dotted with prefelt snake slices. Prefelt snakes are fun to make, and they are a great way to use leftover roving. When you slice them, you see rings of color, sometimes colors you forgot were in there!

Directions

Making the felt inlay

1. Following steps 1 to 6 on pages 12–13, arrange the white wool roving to cover most of the reed mat.

2. Follow steps 1 to 4 of the felting stage on page 13.

3. Remove the net. Arrange prefelt, diagonal-cut snake slices randomly on the wet fiber layers. Using the squirt bottle, wet the slices and gently press them into place.

4. Cover the layers with the net and rub for fifteen minutes, adding soapy water as necessary.

5. Follow steps 1 to 6 of the fulling stage on page 15.

Making a prefelt snake

1. Tease out a wisp of light colored roving, such as yellow or white, and roll it between your palms as if you were making a clay snake. Dip the snake frequently in soapy water. Once it starts to hold its shape, start rolling it on a towel. The fibers should start to felt together but should not reach the fulling stage.

Materials

- felting equipment
- wool roving in assorted colors for prefelt snakes
- wool roving in white
- single-edge razor blade
- rotary cutter, mat, and ruler
- sewing machine
- iron and press cloth
- large snap
- sewing needle and thread
- 12" (30.5 cm) silk ribbon, 1" (2.5 cm) wide

2. Spread out a thin, narrow layer of another color of roving the same length as the beginning snake. Lay the snake in the center of the new color and wrap the new color around it. See photo at right. Add more soapy water and continue rolling the snake on the towel until the new layer takes hold.

3. Continue adding colors as in step 2 until the snake is about the diameter of a nickel and the snake holds its shape. It should still be fuzzy enough that the loose fibers will felt into your felt inlay piece. Let the snake dry completely.

4. Using a single-edge razor, cut slices from the snake, about 1/8" (3 mm) thick. See photo at right. Experiment with different angles, cutting some slices straight across, some diagonally. You can also cut slices in half or into wedges.

Making the glasses case

1. Using the rotary cutter, mat, and ruler, cut two pieces 4" x 7½" (10.2 x 19.1 cm). Round the corners on one end of each rectangle.

2. Place the pieces wrong sides together and machine-stitch with a ⅜" (1 cm) seam on the sides and bottom, leaving the top (straight end) open.

3. Sew the socket part of the snap to the wrong side of the back, about ½" (1.3 cm) below the edge. Sew the ball part of the snap to the wrong side of the front, aligning it to the socket.

4. Tie the ribbon in a bow and hand-tack it near the upper edge of the front. Trim the tails.

TIP: Make a case of a different size to fit your cell phone, MP3 player, or PDA. Never hurts to soften up the hard surfaces of our electronic world!

Materials

- felting equipment
- wool roving in assorted colors for prefelt snakes
- single-edge razor blade
- wool roving in black
- picture frame
- white craft clue
- rotary cutter, mat, and ruler

Picture Frame

Frame a favorite photo with felt inlay and you'll get warm fuzzies every time you look at it. Choose any simple picture frame with wide flat sides. Then design your felt inlay to accent the photo. This black felt with inlaid prefelt snake slices really shows off a black and white print.

Directions

Making the felt inlay

1. Make a prefelt snake, following the directions on page 46. Cut the snake into thin slices.

2. Following steps 1 to 6 on pages 12–13, arrange the black wool roving to cover most of the reed mat.

3. Follow steps 1 to 4 of the felting stage on page 13.

4. Remove the net. Arrange the prefelt snake slices randomly on the wet fiber layers. Using the squirt bottle, wet the slices and gently press them into place.

5. Cover the layers with the net and rub for fifteen minutes, adding soapy water as necessary.

6. Follow steps 1 to 6 of the fulling stage on page 15.

Making the frame

1. Using the rotary cutter, mat, and ruler, cut strips of felt inlay to cover the frame sides.

2. Glue the felt inlay strips to the frame, abutting the edges.

TIP: If you want to avoid abutting cut edges, lay the empty frame facedown on the felt and trace around the outside and opening with chalk. Then cut the piece to fit. Save the center scrap for future projects.

PENCIL ROVING INLAYS

Pencil roving is wool fibers felted into a loose cord about the diameter of a pencil. It is sold ready-to-use in 1-yd. (0.91 m) lengths, in a variety of colors. Because pencil roving has not been processed through the fulling stage, you inlay it into your felt the same way you do with prefelts.

Use pencil roving to inlay simple line drawings, plaids, coils, or spirals in felt pieces. Accent felt beads and snakes with pencil roving squiggles. Keep in mind that the pencil roving is likely to shift a little during the felting and don't expect precise results.

Daisy Coasters

Jazz up your next patio party with these brightly colored coasters. Make an entire set of matching coasters or work on two different colors at a time and make an extra set to give to a friend. Your pencil roving daisy shapes will migrate a little, giving each one unique character.

Directions

Making the inlay

1. Following steps 1 to 6 on pages 12–13, arrange the wool roving to cover most of the reed mat. If you want to make two colors at once, leave a space between them so they won't felt together.

2. Follow steps 1 to 4 of the felting stage on page 13.

3. Remove the net. Visually divide your space: you should be able to get six coasters out of a single sheet of felt or two coasters out of each half sheet, if you are making two colors at once. Arrange a small circle of pencil roving for the center of each daisy. Then arrange five loops for petals, using a diameter of about 3½" (8.9 cm) for each. Add a green loop leaf to each daisy. Using the squirt bottle, wet the designs and gently press them into place.

4. Cover the layers with the net and rub for fifteen minutes, adding soapy water as necessary.

5. Follow steps 1 to 6 of the fulling stage on page 15.

(continued)

Materials

- felting equipment
- wool roving in desired colors for background
- pencil roving in various colors, including green
- thin sheet of cork
- iron and press cloth
- circle template
- sharp scissors
- fabric adhesive

Daisy Coasters (continued)

Making the coasters

1. If your cork came on a roll, set your iron to medium heat. Using a press cloth, press the cork until it is flat.

2. Using a circle template, trace 3½" (8.9 cm) circles on the cork and cut them out with sharp scissors.

3. Center the circle template over a daisy and cut it out. Repeat for each daisy.

4. Spread adhesive on the cork circle and glue it to the back of a daisy circle. Repeat for each coaster.
Trim the coasters as necessary.

TIP: Don't have a compass for drawing a circle?
Use the bottom of a mug or a food can as a guide.

Snake Necklace

Snake Necklace

Drape this snake around your neck and others will gasp—not from shock but in awe of your creativity. Here's your chance to have some fun with colorful felt snake chunks, pencil roving, and beaded embellishments.

Directions

Making the necklace

1. Divide a 1-yd. (0.91 m) length of roving in half lengthwise. Set one piece aside for another step.

2. Dip the roving in the soap solution. Lay one end across the bamboo mat and fold the mat over it. Roll the area back and forth to make the roving felt together. Check your progress frequently and add more soapy water, if necessary.

3. Move the roving so the opposite end is between the mat layers. Roll it back and forth to make it felt.

4. Shift the position of the roving as you continue to roll the mat until a dense felt snake of fairly even diameter forms.

5. Spiral-wrap white pencil roving around the felt snake from one end to the other. You may need two or three lengths of pencil roving.

6. Wet down the pencil roving and rub the snake gently between your hands until the pencil roving begins to cling to the snake.

Materials

- felting equipment
- hand-painted wool roving in pink, green, and orange color range
- white pencil roving
- sewing needle and thread
- pink beads in various sizes and shapes
- beading needle and thread
- round-nose pliers
- two gold end caps
- two gold jump rings
- two gold head pins
- gold clasp
- white craft glue

7. Put the snake back between layers of the mat and finish the fulling process to make the necklace. Cut the necklace to the desired length.

8. Make a short snake from some of the remaining colored roving. Do not add the pencil roving to this piece. Let it dry.

9. From the second snake, cut three 1" (2.5 cm) felt "beads" and one ½" (1.3 cm) felt bead. With a sewing needle and thread, stitch a 1" (2.5 cm) felt bead to the center of the necklace; stitch a ½" (1.3 cm) felt bead to the center of the first felt bead. Stitch the other two felt beads to the necklace ½" (1.3 cm) from each side of the center felt bead.

10. With the beading thread and needle, stitch beads of various sizes to the felt beads and to the necklace in the area around the felt beads.

11. Put a head pin into the large hole in an end cap and out through the small hole. Trim the pin, leaving 1" (2.5 cm) extending from the end cap. Using round-nose pliers, make a loop in the head pin close to the end cap. Repeat for the other end cap and head pin.

12. Half fill an end cap with glue and push one end of the necklace into the glue. Repeat for the other end.

13. Attach the clasp pieces with jump rings to the loops in the end caps.

TIP: Make a matching bracelet with the remaining roving but omit the felt beads. Instead, scatter seed beads or sew them on to follow the trail of the pencil roving.

Materials

- felting equipment
- hand-painted wool roving in blue to green to brown color range
- pencil roving in black, light blue, and yellow
- rotary cutter, mat, and ruler
- vinyl checkbook cover
- white craft glue and brush
- fabric shears

Plaid Checkbook Cover

Transform a cheap vinyl checkbook cover into an elegant fashion accessory. Create a stir at the cashier counter when you whip out your one-of-a-kind felt plaid checkbook. Even bill-paying time will become more enjoyable.

Directions

Making the felt inlay

1. Following steps 1 to 6 on pages 12–13, arrange the wool roving to cover most of the reed mat.

2. Follow steps 1 to 4 of the felting stage on page 13.

3. Remove the net. Arrange pencil roving in a plaid pattern, using all three colors. Keep in mind that the pattern will distort slightly but that's the beauty of the craft! Using the squirt bottle, wet the pencil roving and gently press it into place.

4. Cover the layers with the net and rub gently for fifteen minutes, adding soapy water as necessary.

5. Follow steps 1 to 6 of the fulling stage on page 15.

Making the checkbook cover

1. Using the rotary cutter, mat, and ruler, trim and square up one long side and one short side of the inlay.

2. Brush glue on one side of the checkbook cover and line up the edges to the squared corner of the felt.

3. With the cover closed, spread glue on the rest of the checkbook cover and press the felt in place.

4. Using fabric shears, trim away excess felt.

5. Place the checkbook cover under a heavy book until the glue dries.

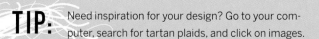
TIP: Need inspiration for your design? Go to your computer, search for tartan plaids, and click on images.

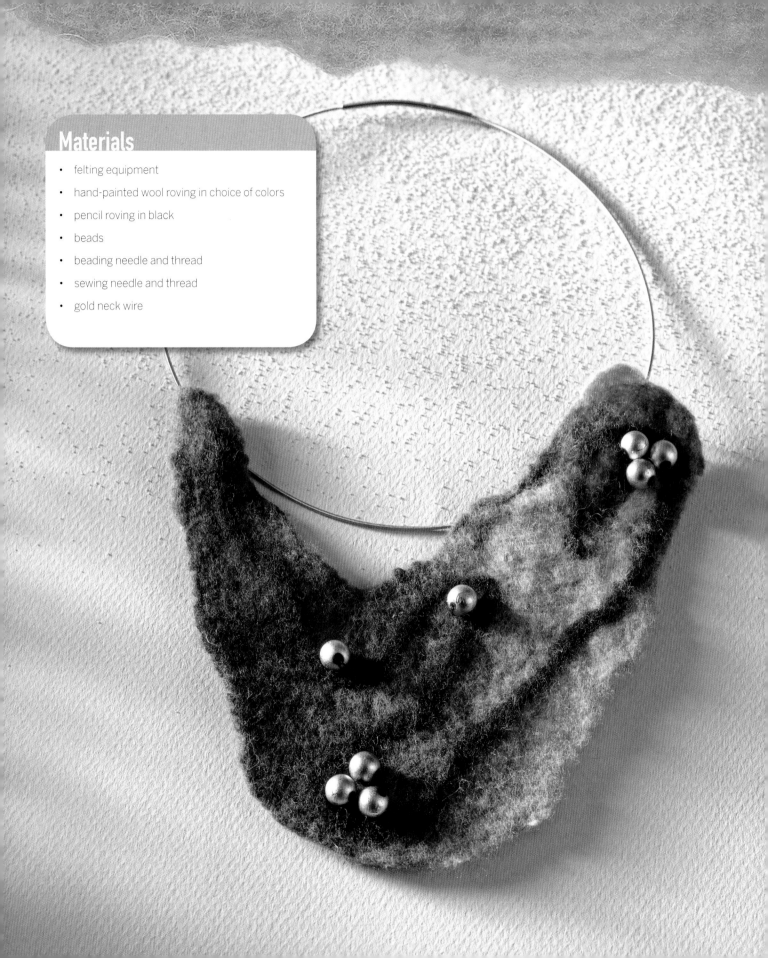

Freeform Necklace

You can't mess up a freeform necklace. By its very nature, it is an artistic experiment and a work of art all rolled into one. Blend some leftover roving scraps to create dramatic color. Add an expressive trail of pencil roving. Finish it off with a scatter of beads.

Directions

Making the felt inlay

1. Arrange three layers of roving in alternating directions, forming a loose V shape.

2. Follow steps 1 to 4 of the felting stage on pages 12–13.

3. Remove the net. Arrange the pencil roving in an expressive swish. Using the squirt bottle, wet the pencil roving and gently press it into place.

4. Cover the layers with the net and rub gently for fifteen minutes, adding soapy water as necessary.

5. Follow steps 1 to 6 of the fulling stage on page 15. Every time you open the roll and move the piece you can encourage the shape you want.

Making the necklace

1. Using the beading needle and thread, stitch beads to the felt inlay in artistic placement.

2. Hand-stitch the felt inlay to the gold neck wire.

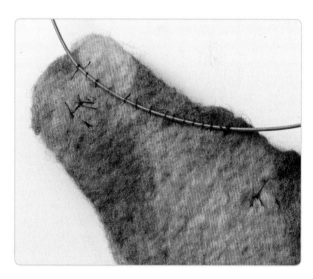

TIP: Use other kinds of inlays to make similar necklaces. Create prefelt designs and embellish them with embroidery stitches.

SILK INLAYS

Silk roving is fun to work with and the fibers bring a wonderful sheen to your designs. Most fiber shops carry silk roving in many solid or hand-painted colors. Besides roving, silk comes in several other forms that can be incorporated into felt inlays, including silk hankies, silk paper, and a by-product of silk fabric manufacturing called throwsters waste. These are the scraggly ends that are cut away—trash to manufacturers but treasure to fiber artists!

Rose Garden Needle Book

This dainty needle book is the perfect place to keep track of sewing needles. Lustrous silk fibers are inlaid in the felt and the book cover is beautifully accented with silk ribbon embroidery. Wouldn't this make a great gift for a special quilter or embroiderer in your life?

Directions

Making the felt inlay

1. Following steps 1 to 6 on pages 12–13, arrange the wool roving to cover most of the reed mat.

2. Follow steps 1 to 4 of the felting stage on page 13.

3. Remove the net. Tease fine wisps of silk fibers from the silk roving and arrange them over the wet layers. Using the squirt bottle, wet the silk fibers and gently press them into place.

4. Cover the layers with the net and rub gently for fifteen minutes, adding soapy water as necessary.

5. Follow steps 1 to 6 of the fulling stage on page 15.

(continued)

Materials

- felting equipment
- hand-painted wool roving in gold to purple color range
- silk roving in red to purple color range
- rotary cutter, mat, and ruler
- craft felt in off-white
- sewing machine and thread
- silk ribbon for embroidery, ⅛" (3 mm) wide, in pink and green
- embroidery needle
- iron and press cloth

Rose Garden Needle Book (continued)

Making the needle book

1. Using the rotary cutter, mat, and ruler, cut a 4" x 5¾" (10.2 x 14.6 cm) rectangle for the needle book cover.

2. Machine-stitch around the felt piece ⅜" (1 cm) seam. Then stitch two rows vertically and four rows horizontally, dividing the surface into a grid. The lines need not be straight or equally spaced.

3. Cut two pieces of craft felt 3" x 4½" (7.6 x 11.4 cm) for needle pages. Layer the pages and fold them in half to find the center. Center the pages on the wrong side of the book cover, and stitch them down the middle. Fold the book in half and press, using a press cloth.

4. Using the silk ribbon embroidery techniques opposite, stitch spider web roses in the center of some of the spaces on the book front. Add ribbon stitch leaves next to the roses.

5. To make the ties, cut a 10" (25.4 cm) piece of each ribbon color. Thread both ends of one piece through the needle eye, and stitch them through the felt at the center of one side, ⅛" (3 mm) from the edge. Remove the needle and pull the ribbon ends through the loop. Pull tight. Repeat for the opposite side, using the other ribbon. Tie tiny knots near the ribbon ends.

TIP: Apply hand lotion a few minutes before handling silk roving to prevent the fibers from clinging to your fingers.

5

Silk ribbon embroidery techniques

Spider web rose. Using embroidery floss or thread, stitch five evenly spaced, ¼" (6 mm) spokes, originating from the center of an imaginary circle. Tie off the thread. Thread the needle with ribbon, knot the end, and bring it to the right side at the center of the spokes. Weave the ribbon over and under the spokes in a circle, working gradually outward, until the spokes are covered. Keep the ribbon loose and allow it to twist occasionally. Push the needle through to the back and secure it.

Ribbon stitch. Knot the end and bring the ribbon to the right side of the fabric. Smooth the ribbon flat against the fabric in the direction of the stitch. Insert the needle at the end of the stitch, piercing the center of the ribbon. Pull the needle through to the underside until the ribbon curls inward at the tip. Secure.

TIP: If you don't want to embroider the silk ribbon roses, you could embellish your needle book with flower beads or purchased ribbon flowers.

Victorian Clutch

Silk hankies aren't for dabbing tears. They are gossamer-thin layers of silk fibers loosely matted together. Purchased as a bundle of squares, they can be used individually or more than one at a time. Silk hankies are off-white and can be dyed or painted. As you can see by this small Victorian clutch, they will inlay with wool fibers beautifully.

Directions

Making the felt inlay

1. Following steps 1 to 6 on pages 12–13, arrange the wool roving to cover most of the reed mat.

2. Follow steps 1 to 4 of the felting stage on page 13.

3. Remove the net. Separate one silk hankie from the bundle and lay it on the wet fibers. Using the squirt bottle, wet the silk fibers and gently press them into place.

4. Cover the layers with the net and rub gently for fifteen minutes, adding soapy water as necessary.

5. Follow steps 1 to 6 of the fulling stage on page 15.

6. Apply gold fabric paint to the inlaid hankie very sparingly to give it a rich, antique look. Allow it to dry.

Materials

- felting equipment
- wool roving in purple
- silk hankie
- gold textile paint
- artist's paintbrush
- rotary cutter, mat, and ruler
- sewing machine
- assorted gold antique buttons
- lavender octagon beads, 5mm
- beading thread and needle
- sewing needle and thread
- iron and press cloth

(continued)

Victorian Clutch (continued)

Making the clutch

1. Using the rotary cutter, mat, and ruler, cut a rectangle of felt 10" x 6½" (25.4 x 16.5 cm). Leave one short end with its natural edge for the flap.

2. Fold in the straight-cut short end 3½" (8.9 cm), wrong sides together. Machine-stitch the sides with a 3/8" (1 cm) seam. Turn the flap down and press the clutch, using a press cloth.

3. Select a large button for the closure. Cut a slit in the center of the flap, ½" (1.3 cm) from the edge, just long enough to fit over the button. Stitch the button to the clutch, aligning it to the slit.

4. Hand-stitch the remaining buttons and the lavender beads randomly to the flap.

Cell Phone Bag

Cell Phone Bag

This cushy, classy cell phone bag is made from felt inlaid with throwsters waste. Throwsters waste is a tangle of silk threads that have been cut from silk fabrics by the manufacturer. They come in a variety of vibrant colors. In the resource list on page 96, you will find a source for throwsters waste. Some stores that carry specialty fibers may also have throwsters waste. Once you try them, you'll find lots of uses for them, too.

Directions

Making the felt inlay

1. Following steps 1 to 6 on pages 12–13, arrange the blue wool roving on the reed mat.

2. Follow steps 1 to 4 of the felting stage on page 13.

3. Remove the net. Tease small wisps of fiber from the clump of throwsters waste and scatter them randomly on the wet fibers. Using the squirt bottle, wet the silk fibers and gently press them into place.

4. Cover the layers with the net and rub gently for fifteen minutes, adding soapy water as necessary.

5. Follow steps 1 to 6 of the fulling stage on page 15.

Materials

- felting equipment
- wool roving in royal blue
- throwsters waste in jewel tones
- rotary cutter, mat, and ruler
- sewing machine and thread
- sewing needle and thread
- large snap

Making the cell phone bag

1. Using the rotary cutter, mat, and ruler, cut two 4" x 5½" (10.1 x 14 cm) pieces.

2. With the sewing machine, quilt vertical lines ⅝" (1.6 cm) apart on each piece.

3. Place the pieces right sides together. Machine-stitch the sides and bottom with a ⅜" (1 cm) seam, rounding the corners.

4. Turn the bag right side out. On the inside, just below the opening, sew the ball and socket of the snap to opposite sides of the bag.

TIP: Cell phones come in different sizes. Before you cut, make sure these measurements will accommodate your phone. Or use this same idea in appropriate measurements to make a case for an ultra-thin digital camera, a magnifying glass, or a handheld mirror.

Starry Sky Address Book

What was once a ho-hum address book is now a stunning desktop accessory. For this project, you first make a thin sheet of silk paper, using silk roving fibers in a process called silk fusion. Star shapes, cut from the silk paper, are inlaid into a deep blue felt sky to create the new book cover.

Directions

Making the silk paper

1. Lay the net on the waxed paper or plastic. Arrange the silk fibers in three thin layers as you would lay out wool roving to make felt, coving half of the net fabric. Fold the net fabric over the fibers.

2. Make a shampoo solution of ¼ tsp. of shampoo to 1 cup (240 mL) of water. Gently paint the net fabric with the shampoo solution, first on one side and then on the other, thoroughly soaking the fibers.

3. With the sponge, blot the excess water and soap.

4. Paint the textile medium on the fibers through the net, first on one side and then on the other, thoroughly soaking the fibers. Lay out to dry.

5. Carefully remove the net. The silk paper is ready to use.

Materials

- wax paper or plastic
- net fabric
- silk roving in gold
- shampoo without conditioner
- paintbrush
- sponge
- textile medium
- felting equipment
- wool roving in medium blue, pale blue, and pale lavender
- rotary cutter, mat, and ruler
- iron and press cloth
- small address book
- fabric adhesive

(continued)

Starry Sky Address Book (continued)

Making the felt inlay

1. Following steps 1 to 6 on pages 12–13, arrange the blue wool roving on the reed mat. Add thin diagonal rows of pale blue and lavender roving.

2. Follow steps 1 to 4 of the felting stage on page 13.

3. Remove the net. Cut stars from the silk paper and scatter them over the wet layers. Using the squirt bottle, wet the silk fibers and gently press them into place.

4. Cover the layers with the net and rub gently for fifteen minutes, adding soapy water as necessary.

5. Follow steps 1 to 6 of the fulling stage on page 15.

Covering the address book

1. Cut the felt inlay to cover the front, back, and spine of the address book.

2. Apply adhesive to the covers and spine of the address book. Adhere the felt.

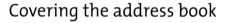

TIP: Here's a quick, easy way to make silk paper: Crease a piece of parchment paper down the center and lay it on your work surface. Lay out three layers of silk fibers on half of the paper. Spray starch on the fibers. Flip over and spray the second side. Fold the paper over the fibers. With an iron set to medium heat, press until the fibers are dry.

MORE POSSIBILITIES

Experiment with other fibers and fabrics in your felt inlays. You never know how well something works until you try it. For example, scrim—a cotton gauze fabric like cheesecloth— will inlay very easily on the wool fibers.

Various other natural fibers, such as mohair, camel hair, alpaca, cashmere, and llama, work well. Even silk ribbons can be inlaid into your felt.

Materials

- felting equipment
- hand-painted wool roving in peach to beige to green color range
- scrim in mossy green
- earth-tone beads of various sizes and shapes
- pillow
- sewing needle and thread

Mossy Rock Pillow

An experiment with scrim resulted in this very organic inlay that looks like moss growing on a slab of granite. A few beads added texture and the felt inlay became a decorative accent for a pillow.

Directions

Making the felt inlay

1. Following steps 1 to 6 on pages 12–13, arrange the wool roving to cover most of the reed mat.

2. Follow steps 1 to 4 of the felting stage on page 13.

3. Remove the net. Arrange scrim pieces on top of the wet layers. Using the squirt bottle, wet the scrim and gently press it into place.

4. Cover the layers with the net and rub gently for fifteen minutes, adding soapy water as necessary.

5. Follow steps 1 to 6 of the fulling stage on page 15.

Embellishing the pillow

1. Leave the felt inlay in its natural shape. Sew beads in small clusters to the felt inlay.

2. Center the felt inlay on the pillow front and hand-stitch it to the pillow around the edge.

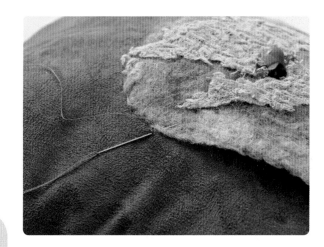

TIP: You may have to rub longer to get the wool fibers to hook onto the scrim fabric, but the results are very interesting. Try overlaying some of the scrim edges with more wool fibers to help lock the scrim in place.

Beaded Barrette

You've been saving all of your felt inlay scraps, right? Beaded barrettes will help you make good use of them. Choose a scrap that has some interesting color and texture variations and then have some fun with embellishments.

Directions

Making the barrette

1. Using the rotary cutter, mat, and ruler, cut a piece of felt inlay to match the surface of the barrette.

2. Sew beads in various patterns throughout the felt inlay.

3. Glue the felt inlay piece to the barrette.

Materials

- felt inlay scraps
- flat spring-closure barrette
- rotary cutter, mat, and ruler
- assorted beads to accent the felt colors
- beading needle and thread
- fabric adhesive

TIP: Use this idea to embellish other plain fashion accessories, like wide headbands or wristbands. Change an ordinary tin can into a spectacular desk accessory. Almost any flat surface is fair game.

Mohair Headband

Mohair is a curly fiber from a goat. It will inlay well and is soft and silky. It gives the felt a very elegant feel. Use the fibers sparingly and let them keep their natural curl.

Directions

Making the felt inlay

1. Following steps 1 to 6 on pages 12–13, arrange the purple wool roving on the reed mat to cover an area 2" (5.1 cm) wider and longer than the surface of the headband.

2. Follow steps 1 to 4 of the felting stage on page 13.

3. Remove the net. Arrange wisps of mohair roving on the wet layers. Using the squirt bottle, wet the mohair and gently press it into place.

4. Cover the layers with the net and rub gently for fifteen minutes, adding soapy water as necessary.

5. Follow steps 1 to 6 of the fulling stage on page 15. When you turn it, stretch the strip gently to help it keep its shape

(continued)

Materials

- felting equipment
- wool roving in purple and magenta
- mohair in turquoise, blue, and purple
- small plastic bag
- gold seed beads
- beading needle and thread
- plastic headband
- fabric adhesive
- flat glue brush
- fabric shears

TIP: Even for small projects, make your inlay the full size of the mat. You are sure to find uses for leftover pieces of felt inlays.

Making the flowers

1. Pull a wisp of magenta wool from the roving and wrap it around two of your fingers. Place it on the reed mat.

2. Pull a wisp of purple wool from the roving and wrap it around one finger. Place this piece in the center of the magenta circle. Make sure there are no open areas.

3. Repeat steps 1 and 2 to make two more flowers. Wet the flowers, place a net on top, and rub the flowers for about fifteen minutes.

4. Roll up the flowers in the reed mat and roll the mat 200 times.

5. Unroll the mat and rub the flowers some more. When they are completely felted, allow the flowers to dry.

6. Using a beading needle and thread, sew a cluster of seed beads in the center of each flower, and sew the flowers to the felt inlay strip, slightly overlapping.

TIP: Give your fingers a break: rub the net-covered layers with your hands inside plastic bags.

Making the headband

1. Brush the headband with adhesive. Adhere the felt strip.

2. Using fabric shears, trim away the excess felt.

GALLERY

Enjoy the eye candy on the next few pages. These ideas will spark your imagination and help you create many felt inlay masterpieces.

Gallery

Triangle Purse

The inlay for this triangle purse was felted from hand-painted wool roving and inlaid with silk ribbons. Pencil roving was felted to make the strap. An antique button was used for the closure.

Designed by Judy McDowell

Four-Corner Pouch

This four-corner pouch, perfect for holding rings or special earrings, was made from hand-dyed wool roving inlaid with yarn and prefelt patterns. The seams are accented with seed beads.

Designed by Nancy Hoerner

Floral Handbag

Variegated gray wool roving is inlaid with silk throwsters waste and prefelt leaves. The embellishment includes felted snakes, berries, and flowers.

Designed by Nancy Hoerner

Art Doll

The body of this art doll is made from white felt yard goods. Her jacket is felted wool roving with inlays of prefelts and yarn.

Designed by Nancy Hoerner

Patchwork Pillow

When your felting obsession has netted a treasure trove of interesting scraps, make a patchwork pillow.

Designed by Nancy Hoerner

Gallery

Felt Bowls

The inlays for these bowls were formed over various objects, such as a CD or bundled bubble wrap, as they were being felted.

Designed by Nancy Hoerner

Cover Inserts

Metal boxes with glass covers are transformed into art objects when felt inlay scraps are cut and inserted under their covers.

Designed by Nancy Hoerner

Serving Set

Periwinkle and baby blue wool roving were used to make a felted bowl. The flower embellishment is made from the same yarn that was inlaid in the felt. A matching felt inlay is sealed under the glass bottom of a serving tray.

Designed by Nancy Hoerner

Buttoned Cluch

Pink and blue hand-painted wool roving were inlaid with silk ribbons to make this clutch-style handbag.

Designed by Judy McDowell

About the Author

Nancy Hoerner is an accomplished artist and designer, who has been developing her artwork for the past thirty years. She has published art dolls and bead projects in nationally known magazines and studied doll making and beading with renowned artists. Many of her art dolls and beadwork are held in private collections. Nancy also works with manufacturers in the craft industry.

Acknowledgments

I would like to thank my friend and teacher Judy McDowell for sharing her knowledge and inspiration with me. Without Judy, I would not have come this far. Please visit her website www.mistymeadowicelandics.com.

I would also like to thank Linda and Barbara for their continuing support and friendship.

Thanks to Pep for all of his proofreading and his continuing support.

Resources

Colorful Quilts and Textiles
www.colorfulquiltsandtextiles.com
(651) 628-6644
fused glass buttons; hand-painted merino roving; textile medium
for silk paper; silk hankies, rods, tops, and cocoons in color packs

Misty Meadow
www.mistymeadowicelandics.com
(952) 472-0883
Icelandic wool

Chris Hanner and Company
www.myfavoritethimble.com
(770) 979-1055
pencil roving, felting needles

Outback Fibers
www.outbackfibers.com
(800) 276-5015
throwsters waste, prefelt fabric, silk hankies